First World War
and Army of Occupation
War Diary
France, Belgium and Germany

59 DIVISION
177 Infantry Brigade
Leicestershire Regiment
2/5th Battalion
7 January 1916 - 29 February 1916

WO95/3022/5

The Naval & Military Press Ltd
www.nmarchive.com
Published in association with The National Archives

Published by

The Naval & Military Press Ltd

Unit 10 Ridgewood Industrial Park,

Uckfield, East Sussex,

TN22 5QE England

Tel: +44 (0) 1825 749494

www.naval-military-press.com

www.nmarchive.com

This diary has been reprinted in facsimile from the original. Any imperfections are inevitably reproduced and the quality may fall short of modern type and cartographic standards.

© Crown Copyright
Images reproduced by permission of The National Archives, London, England, 2015.

Contents

Document type	Place/Title	Date From	Date To
Heading	WO95/3022/5 1916 Jan-Feb 2/5 Battalion Leicestershire Regiment		
Heading	War Diary Of 2/5 Bn Leicestershire Regt. From Jan 1st 1916 To 31st 1916		
War Diary	Harpenden	07/01/1916	27/01/1916
Heading	War Diary Of 2/5 Battalion The Leicestershire Regiment From Feb 1st 1916-Feb 29 1916		
War Diary	Harpenden	02/02/1916	29/02/1916

WO/95/3022/5

1916 Jan-Feb

2/5 Battalion Leicestershire Regiment.

Confidential

War Diary
of
2/5¹ Bⁿ Leicestershire Regᵗ

from Jan 1ˢᵗ 1916.
to — 31ˢᵗ 1916.

E. C. Atkins Lᵗ Col
2/5 Bⁿ Leicestershire Regᵗ

2/5 BN. THE LEICESTERSHIRE REGT.

Army Form C. 2118.

WAR DIARY
or
INTELLIGENCE SUMMARY
(Erase heading not required.)

Instructions regarding War Diaries and Intelligence Summaries are contained in F.S. Regs., Part II. and the Staff Manual respectively. Title pages will be prepared in manuscript.

HEADQUARTERS 177th INFANTRY BRIGADE
8 – FEB 1916
No. ....

Hour, Date, Place	Summary of Events and Information	Remarks and references to Appendices
7/1/16 HARPENDEN	Command of Brigade taken over by BRIGADIER GENERAL C.G. BLACKADER D.S.O.	
13/1/16 HARPENDEN	Division came under command of G.O.C. 3rd Army and ceased to be under G.O.C.-in-C. CENTRAL FORCE.	
22/1/16 HARPENDEN	Draft of 21 Reservist Recruits, called up under LORD DERBY'S Scheme, taken on strength	
24/1/16 HARPENDEN	Further Draft of 20 Recruits arrived	
26/1/16 HARPENDEN	Further Draft of 86 Recruits arrived	
27/1/16 HARPENDEN	Further Draft of 43 Recruits arrived	

E.C. Lewis Lt.Col

Confidential

War Diary
of the
2/5 Battalion
The
Leicestershire Regiment

from Feb 1st 1916 — Feb 29. 1916.

2/5 Leicestershire Regt.

WAR DIARY
or
INTELLIGENCE SUMMARY.
(Erase heading not required.)

Army Form C. 2118.

Instructions regarding War Diaries and Intelligence Summaries are contained in F.S. Regs., Part II. and the Staff Manual respectively. Title pages will be prepared in manuscript.

Hour, Date, Place	Summary of Events and Information	Remarks and references to Appendices
2/2/16 HARPENDEN	General SIR A.E. CODRINGTON inspected Bde on route March, troops passing him near REDBOURNE.	RPS
14/2/16 HARPENDEN	MAJOR GENERAL A.E. SANDBACH C.B. D.S.O Taken over command of Division from this date.	RPS
9 pm 29/2/16 HARPENDEN	Orders received for Division to prepare to move. Test only. Columns paraded, and were inspected by G.O.C. Bde.	RPS

(73989) W4141—463. 400,000. 9/14. H.&J.Ltd. Forms/C. 2118/10.

www.ingramcontent.com/pod-product-compliance
Lightning Source LLC
Chambersburg PA
CBHW081516160426
43193CB00014B/2706